W9-BLM-166

BRIDGET "BIDDY" MASON

FROM SLAVE TO BUSINESSWOMAN

BRIDGET "BIDDY"
MASON
FROM SLAVE TO BUSINESSWOMAN

By Jean Kinney Williams

Content Adviser: Melodie Andrews, Ph.D.,
Associate Professor of Early American
and Women's History
Minnesota State University, Mankato

Reading Adviser: Rosemary G. Palmer, Ph.D.,
Department of Literacy, College of Education,
Boise State University

COMPASS POINT BOOKS MINNEAPOLIS, MINNESOTA

Compass Point Books
3109 West 50th Street, #115
Minneapolis, MN 55410

Visit Compass Point Books on the Internet at *www.compasspointbooks.com*
or e-mail your request to *custserv@compasspointbooks.com*

Editors: Sue Vander Hook and Nick Healy
Lead Designer: Jaime Martens
Photo Researcher: Marcie C. Spence
Page Production: The Design Lab, Bobbie Nuytten
Cartographer: XNR Productions, Inc.
Educational Consultant: Diane Smolinski

Managing Editor: Catherine Neitge
Creative Director: Keith Griffin
Editorial Director: Carol Jones

Library of Congress Cataloging-in-Publication Data
Williams, Jean Kinney.
 Bridget "Biddy" Mason : from slave to businesswoman / by Jean Kinney
Williams.
    p. cm.—(Signature lives)
 Includes bibliographical references and index.
 ISBN-13: 978-0-7565-1001-5 (hardcover)
 ISBN-10: 0-7565-1001-5 (hardcover)
 ISBN-13: 978-0-7565-1843-1 (paperback)
 ISBN-10: 0-7565-1843-1 (paperback)
 1. Mason, Biddy, 1818-1891—Juvenile literature. 2. Women slaves—
United States—Biography—Juvenile literature. 3. Slaves—United
States—Biography—Juvenile literature. 4. African American women—
Biography—Juvenile literature. 5. African American midwives—
California—Biography—Juvenile literature. I. Title. II. Series.
 E444.M38W55 2006
 973'.0496073'0092—dc22   2005002745

Signature Lives

AMERICAN FRONTIER ERA

By the late 1700s, the United States was growing into a nation of homesteaders, politicians, mountain men, and American dreams. Manifest Destiny propelled settlers to push west, conquering and "civilizing" from coast to coast. In keeping with this vision, world leaders hammered out historic agreements such as the Louisiana Purchase, which drastically increased U.S. territory. This ambition often led to bitter conflicts with Native Americans trying to protect their way of life and their traditional lands. Life on the frontier was often filled with danger and difficulties. The people who wove their way into American history overcame these challenges with a courage and conviction that defined an era and shaped a nation.

Table of Contents

Chapter
1   FREE FOREVER

❧⟡❧

The poor but determined slave woman called Biddy waited at the courthouse in Los Angeles, California. The sunrise that January morning in 1856 brought with it the possibility of freedom. An important court hearing was due to enter its second day in that tiny Western town. Biddy's future was at stake.

The hearing pitted Biddy against Robert M. Smith, the man who had been her owner for years. Smith intended to move Biddy, along with his family and the rest of his slaves, to Texas. Unlike California, Texas was a state where slavery was legal. Biddy hoped to stay in California, where she might be free, but the judge would have to decide.

Trouble started even before the second day of

Los Angeles was a small town when Biddy arrived there in the 1850s.

the hearing could begin. Biddy's lawyer did not show up in court, and Biddy could not proceed on her own. State law would not allow it. Although California was a free state, a law there made it illegal for a black person, or anyone who was not white, to testify in court against a white person. Without her lawyer, Biddy—who would someday become one of the most successful women in all of the West—had no way to make her voice be heard.

It may seem strange that California or any free state would have such a law. But in fact, that law serves as an example of how deeply confused and divided Americans were on matters of race. Millions of black people lived in slavery, and even those blacks in free states were not fully free. Laws like the one in California made black people second-class citizens. A federal law called the Fugitive Slave Act was causing a great deal of worry not only for escaped slaves living in the North but also for free blacks everywhere.

By the time Biddy found herself in a California courtroom, disputes over the future of slavery had been occurring in the United States for decades. Years earlier, the free states of the North and the slave states of the South had reached a sort of balance. The U.S. Senate, which had two lawmakers from each state, was split evenly between slavery's supporters and its opponents. Neither side had

An overseer on horseback watches slaves at work in a cotton field.

enough power to change laws regarding slavery. Northern lawmakers could not limit slavery without the votes of Southerners. Lawmakers from the South could not expand slavery without the votes of Northerners. Now, the westward growth of the nation threatened to throw off that balance.

Southern lawmakers fought to protect slavery. They pushed to allow slavery in new states. As far back as 1820, they forced a series of new laws and compromises that protected slavery and kept millions of blacks enslaved. California became a state in 1850 after a major compromise between pro- and

11

antislavery forces. The deal made California a free state, but left the issue of slavery open in the regions that are now New Mexico, Arizona, Utah, and Nevada.

The compromise also changed the nation's law regarding escaped slaves. The 1850 Fugitive Slave Act meant escaped slaves would no longer be safe in the free North. It also meant free blacks faced the danger of being mistaken for an escaped slave. They could be captured and sent to live in slavery without a chance to prove their identity.

The legal battle over Biddy seems like a small dispute, considering the nationwide conflict over slavery and all the powerful people on both sides. After all, Biddy was just one person, and a slave at that. Her life had begun quietly, far from California and far from the spotlight.

She was born 37 years earlier in Georgia and moved to Mississippi with her owners, who were seeking better cropland. As a young woman, she became the property of Smith and his wife, Rebecca. She labored for the Smiths, caring for their children and watching over their livestock. Forced to journey with them as they uprooted their family and headed west, Biddy traveled thousands of miles, and she walked most of the way. Finally, she spent nearly five years in California, where the law said she could be free but where the Smiths

An 1850 illustration shows the effects of the Fugitive Slave Act.

forced her to live like a slave.

Now Smith planned to take her to Texas, where freedom would be far from her reach. A last-minute legal challenge had protected her in California long enough for Judge Benjamin Hayes to consider her case and to determine whether her owner should be allowed to proceed with his plan. Curious townspeople flocked to the courthouse for the hearing. Even *The New York Times* sent a reporter to cover the story.

When it became clear Biddy's lawyer was not coming, the judge had decisions to make. Smith's lawyer called for Hayes to dismiss the matter and return Biddy to her owner. California law said Biddy

---

Although people of African descent were a small minority in the early history of California, they made important contributions. Of the 44 people who founded Los Angeles in 1781, 26 were African-Americans. A child of those first black pioneers, Maria Rita Valdez Villa, grew up to become the "owner" of Beverly Hills. Her ranch sprawled across that valuable land from 1838 until she sold it in 1854.

could not speak up in the courtroom where her own fate was being debated. Biddy's hopes seemed dim, but the judge did something unexpected. He called Biddy into his office and interviewed her there. California had no law against that. Hayes had found a way to hear Biddy's side of things. She explained herself to the judge, and returned to the jailhouse across the alley, where the judge had placed her and Smith's other slaves for their own protection.

The next day, Hayes read his decision to the packed courtroom: All of Robert Smith's slaves were "entitled to their freedom and are free forever."

Biddy, who soon took the last name Mason, began her new life with little more than her hopes and the clothes on her back. She stayed put in California, where she continued to be swept up in the growth of the American West. She saw Los Angeles transform from a dusty town into a thriving city. She proved to be a pioneer of sorts. Although she never learned to read or write, she became the

The first Los Angeles jail and city hall became a railroad ticket and real estate office.

first black woman to own property in the city. She built a personal fortune that made her among the area's wealthiest people.

Her investments in real estate proved to be wise. Land she bought cheap soared in value as the city grew around it. Yet Biddy did not drastically change her way of living. She continued to care for people in need, to help new mothers and their children, and to watch out for her neighbors.

Today, Los Angeles is the second-largest city in the United States, and Biddy's legacy remains important there. Her journey from slavery to freedom and from poverty to wealth continues to inspire others. ✑

2 BORN INTO SLAVERY

❧❀❧

On August 15, 1818, a baby girl was born to a slave woman in Hancock County, Georgia. The birth of a new slave was an everyday occurrence in the Southern states until the time of the Civil War in the 1860s. This infant was named Bridget, but everyone would call her Biddy. It would be many years before she had a last name.

At a very young age, the girl was taken from her parents and moved to the plantation of another slave owner. The fact that this child never really knew her mother or father was not unusual. Slave children and their parents were frequently separated when they were sold and sent to live with different owners, although many slaveholders believed this practice was wrong.

A map of Georgia around the time of Biddy's birth

Records of Biddy's childhood are unclear and incomplete. It is possible she was sold or given away several times. However, Biddy spent most of her youth on the plantation of a man named John Smithson. Farming was the main source of wealth in the South at the time. Most people owned smaller farms, but some had large farms called plantations. Plantation owners usually owned many slaves to work in the fields.

Biddy shared living quarters with other slaves, who took care of her and taught her how to perform the required tasks. Most slaves in Georgia during the 1800s—whether men, women, or children—worked in fields planting and picking cotton for their owners. There was no time or opportunity for Biddy to learn how to read and write. In fact, it was illegal in most Southern states to teach slaves those basic skills. Slaveholders knew that education was the key to people's ability to advance in life. They believed that denying slaves even a basic education was one more way to keep them under the control of their owners.

Still a child, Biddy was taken by her owner west to Mississippi. Her owner joined the wave of westward movement caused partly by the way people farmed their land. Cotton was the main crop in the South. Busy weaving mills in faraway England bought as much cotton as Southern farmers could grow. But planting cotton year after year in the same area wore out the soil. Many farmers from states such as Georgia or South Carolina had to move west to newer states like Alabama, Mississippi, or Louisiana to find fresh land where they could start new cotton farms.

Biddy knew how to perform a variety of chores such as cooking, cleaning, and doing the laundry. She knew how to take care of livestock such as sheep and cows. As a teenager, she learned these skills from older slaves. Most important, at least for Biddy's future, she learned how to care for people who were ill and to assist women during childbirth.

By the late 1830s, Biddy played an important role on the plantation. Without the help of modern medicine, childbirth was risky and often deadly for mothers and their infants. Biddy could help mother and child through the difficult process. She could also treat others with medicines that she learned to make from roots, plants, and herbs that she raised in a garden or found growing wild. Biddy did not help only her fellow slaves. Black women with her medical skills also treated whites on plantations and often delivered their babies, too.

In the 1840s, Biddy became the property of Robert Smith and his wife, Rebecca Dorn Smith. Some stories say Biddy was given to the Smiths as a wedding present. But records from that time do not make it clear why Biddy went to live with her new owners.

The Smiths had moved away from South Carolina in hopes of having a successful farm on Mississippi's fertile soil. They were not wealthy. They might have been better off getting a strong male slave who could help with farmwork. However, it may have been that Biddy's nursing skills were appealing to the Smiths. Rebecca was sickly and often needed medical care. She also needed a hand with her children, whom Biddy no doubt helped bring into the world. Biddy also could care for the farm animals.

Biddy had three children of her own while she lived in Mississippi. Her first, Ellen, was born in 1838. Another daughter, Ann, was born in 1844 or around that time. Harriet came along in 1847. The identity of the father (or fathers) of Biddy's children remains unknown. Some historians have said that Robert Smith was the father of at least one of the girls.

Biddy and her daughters weren't the only slaves held by the Smiths. In 1846, Rebecca's brother gave them a slave woman named Hannah, who was about 25 years old at the time.

Biddy learned nursing and midwife skills during her earliest days as a slave, beginning in Georgia. The slaves who taught Biddy were passing on healing traditions that came from Africa and the Caribbean, as well as from the Native Americans who lived nearby. Historian Dolores Hayden wrote that medicine from herbs or plant roots was one key. Slave healers "used Jerusalem oak for worms, asafetida for asthma and whooping cough, ... and snakeroot and boneset for malaria." Plants and roots were picked or dug up and then cooked into medicines that were given to the sick in careful doses.

Hannah and Rebecca were not strangers. Years earlier, Hannah had been Rebecca's personal slave, a companion to Rebecca when she was growing up in a wealthy plantation family. Later, after the death of

Rebecca's father, who had been Hannah's owner, all of his slaves had been put up for sale. Rebecca's brother purchased Hannah and her children and gave them to the Smiths.

Like Biddy, Hannah had three children. With the sale of her former owner's slaves, Hannah was now separated from the slave man who had been her companion and who was the father of her children. However, Hannah was fortunate to be able to keep her children with her.

Biddy and Hannah first met when they both lived in Mississippi with the Smiths. They would grow to be friends, and events would link them to each other for years to come.

The Smiths had six children and shared their modest house with Biddy, Hannah, and their children. Robert Smith hadn't found the success he had hoped for in Mississippi. He worked just as hard to scratch a living out of the soil there as he had in South Carolina. But he and Rebecca seemed to find some comfort in a new religion that was winning converts, or new members, from its base in Nauvoo, Illinois, a town located far north on the Mississippi River.

In the early 1840s, members of the Church of Jesus Christ of Latter-day Saints, or Mormons, as they are commonly called, fanned out across the United States. They spread their message about

being chosen by God to lead people to heaven.

The Mormons found a number of converts in Mississippi, including the Smiths. At the time, few African-Americans joined the Mormon church. In general, white Mormons did not believe that black people were their equals. Still, the church would make a big difference in Biddy's life and the lives of all the Smiths' slaves.

The Mormons had become the focus of scorn and suspicion in Illinois. Many other people living near them were afraid the Mormons were trying to

Slaves worked long days planting, weeding, and picking cotton, which was an important crop in the South.

gain too much power in local government and business. Those suspicions were only deepened in early 1844 when Joseph Smith, the leader of the Mormons, announced he wanted to run for president of the United States. (Joseph Smith was not related to Biddy's owners, although they shared the same last name.) Then people heard the Mormons were practicing polygamy, or marriage between a man and more than one woman. This further stirred anger toward the Mormons.

Finally, fighting broke out between church members and their neighbors in and around Nauvoo.

Mormon leader Joseph Smith was killed while being held in the Nauvoo jail.

An angry mob killed Joseph Smith in June 1844, and within a couple of years, the Mormons had to flee the area. They escaped out of Illinois across the Mississippi River and headed west.

Their new leader, Brigham Young, decided to take the Mormons west to the Utah Territory, where the desert baked in the summer sun, where snow fell deep in the winter, and where few other white Americans or

Native Americans wanted to live.

    The church asked all members to go to the Great Salt Lake Basin and help build a new society in the unclaimed desert. Robert and Rebecca Smith were faithful Mormons. They even named one of their sons Joseph after the murdered Mormon leader. However, Robert wanted to move to Texas

An arsonist burned the Mormon Temple at Nauvoo after the Mormons fled to the West.

instead of Utah. He hoped to become a successful farmer in the southern United States.

In 1847, the Smiths packed up their household, including Biddy, Hannah, and their children, and began the long trip toward Texas. When they reached the Mississippi River, it was flooded and too difficult to cross, so they stayed on a rented farm in Mississippi for a year.

Then Robert Smith began hearing talk of gold and beautiful farmland in California. Smith knew he wanted to go there, but first he took his family and slaves to Iowa and Utah, along with thousands of other Mormons.

In March 1848, Robert Smith's household and other Mississippi Mormons met in the northwest part of the state. From there, they began their trek to what they called Winter Quarters, which had been set up on the banks of the Missouri River at the border of Iowa and Nebraska. It would be quite a difficult year of traveling for the group, especially for Biddy and the other slaves. They had to walk most of the way from Mississippi to Winter Quarters and from there to Utah.

Travel was especially difficult for Biddy, whose daughter Harriet was still a baby. Early in the journey, Hannah gave birth to her fourth child and had to care for a newborn as she trekked through the sometimes rugged terrain.

Their travels would take them about 2,000 miles (3,200 kilometers), mostly on foot. As they left Mississippi, Biddy and her children said goodbye forever to the South and headed for a new life in the West.

Bad weather added to the Mormons' troubles as they crossed Iowa.

3 LEAVING THE SOUTH

Chapter

ϾᴥꙄ

Biddy was among 90 people traveling with the wagon train from Mississippi to the Mormons' Winter Quarters. Thirty-four of them were slaves. Smith's party alone had 19 people, including Smith, his wife and six children, another white man who helped drive a wagon, and 10 slaves. Smith also brought along several mules, cows, a horse, and a team of oxen to pull the wagons. Along with watching out for her children, Biddy also had to tend the animals as she walked alongside them.

The Mormon church sent along a guide to lead each group of pioneers to the Iowa-Nebraska border. A man named John Brown traveled with Biddy's group from Mississippi. He wrote down the details of their challenging trip that spring of 1848, as they

A ferry crosses the Missouri River near the Mormons' settlement at Kanesville, Iowa, the site of present-day Council Bluffs.

drove their caravan through Tennessee and Kentucky to the Ohio River.

At the river, they boarded a steamboat hired by the Mormon church to carry its pioneers to the Mississippi River and on up to St. Louis, Missouri. From there, they continued their rugged journey over the land. Cold, rainy weather created roads that were at times so muddy they nearly swallowed up

Steamboats travel on the Ohio River.

the animals. Icy creeks often flooded as winter snows melted. Conditions were often unsanitary, but the people in Biddy's group managed to stay healthy. By the beginning of June 1848, they arrived at Winter Quarters.

Winter Quarters had been settled for about two years. The first Mormons had fled Nauvoo in February 1846, leaving Illinois and crossing over into Iowa. The first group to make the long trip had endured heavy spring rains as they entered Iowa and traveled onward. They headed for the western edge of the state, where they had planned to set up winter camp along the Missouri River.

The land in western Iowa belonged to the Potawatomi Indians, but they gave the Mormons permission to stay on tribal land. The Mormons camped at Kanesville, Iowa, where the city of Council Bluffs is today. Some of them also crossed to the west side of the Missouri River and camped at what is today Omaha, Nebraska.

By the end of 1846, there were

Mormons had been driven out of settlements in Ohio and Missouri before they gathered in Nauvoo, Illinois. Their time in Nauvoo began peacefully, and the Mormons planned to stay. They even began building a grand temple. But in 1844, Mormon leader Joseph Smith was arrested after he shut down a newspaper that had printed damaging allegations about the Mormons. Smith and other church leaders were jailed in Carthage, Illinois. On June 27, an angry mob stormed the jail and killed Smith and his brother, Hyrum.

Covered wagons roll into the settlement at Kanesville, Iowa.

almost 4,000 people at Winter Quarters. Thousands more had settled in and around Kanesville between 1846 and 1848 while waiting to go to Utah.

Many of the first Mormons who arrived in Iowa and Nebraska in 1846 were ill or half-starved after hurrying out of Illinois. During the winter of 1846–1847, they suffered from disease, lack of nutrition, and poor housing conditions. Between June 1846 and October 1848, about 2,000 people died at Winter Quarters.

But the Mormons worked hard to reorganize and make improvements. In the fall of 1846, they surveyed the layout of their settlement and began to develop it more permanently with streets, blocks, lots, and homes. By the time Biddy, Hannah, the Smiths, and the other Mississippians arrived, scores of permanent–looking settlements had sprung up on the eastern bank of the Missouri River.

Robert Smith still thought about heading to California. But those hopes dimmed when the young man who helped him drive the family's wagons died from an accidental shotgun wound. Smith knew he couldn't take his party on a trip like that by himself. With his California hopes dashed for the moment, Smith decided to stay with the Mormons and make plans to travel with them later to the Great Salt Lake Basin.

Biddy and her children didn't have much time to rest or get settled at Winter Quarters. Just about a month after they arrived, the group was ready to leave on the long trip to the West.

The Mormons were divided into three large companies, or groups, that would be led to Utah by Mormon leaders Brigham Young, Heber C. Kimball, and Willard Richards. Young had already

Mormon leader Brigham Young established a new settlement near Utah's Great Salt Lake.

made the trip the year before with the first group of Mormon pioneers.

Now those people were busy building homes, schools, and irrigation systems from local water sources to prepare the dry Utah earth for farming. Young had proposed they name their new settlement after one of the area's natural wonders: the Great Salt Lake. The Mormon encampment soon had the name Salt Lake City.

Biddy and her children were scheduled to cross the Great Plains with the Smith family in the third company. Led by Richards, the group was set to leave in July 1848.

The three companies on the trek to Utah that year consisted of 800 wagons and 2,400 men, women, and children. These adventurous pioneers brought along an assortment of animals, including oxen, cattle, sheep, pigs, chickens, goats, dogs, and cats. Someone even had a pet squirrel. Richards' company had 169 wagons and 525 people. Robert

Smith's household was part of a smaller unit in the company under the direction of Mormon leader John Brown.

On July 7, 1848, the wagon train began its westward journey to a destination about 1,000 miles (1,600 km) away. After little more than a month at Winter Quarters, Biddy and her daughters were on the move again.

The Mormons were very organized, successfully moving huge numbers of people west from Iowa to Utah from 1847 to 1868. The path they took across the Great Plains and mountains became known as the Mormon Trail.

The large flock of converts that made their way west included people from the United States, Canada, England, Sweden, Norway, and Denmark. What happened on that trail and after the group settled in Utah became an important and colorful chapter in the history of the American West, and Biddy Mason was part of it.

There were few black women in the Old West, but those who went there worked hard to enjoy freedom and opportunity. Some of those women lived colorful lives that would have been impossible in the Eastern states. One woman was a stagecoach driver who delivered the mail in Cascade, Montana. Another woman, Cathay Williams, became a successful farmer in the Southwest after serving as a soldier in the 1860s. As a soldier, Williams disguised herself as a man and went by the name William Cathay.

4 ALONG THE MORMON TRAIL

Chapter

❧❧❧

Biddy's long walk west took her into country like she had never seen before. The Mormon Trail followed the Platte River through Nebraska into Wyoming. The Mormon pioneers watched for landmarks with names like Chimney Rock, Scotts Bluffs, and Mitchell Pass. When it was time to cross the Platte River at present-day Casper, Wyoming, a Mormon-operated ferry waited to take people, wagons, and animals to the other side.

Many Mormon travelers kept diaries that described the day-to-day challenges they faced on their journey. They wrote about their wagons breaking down, the sun scorching the people with its heat, and the nighttime temperatures chilling them as summer came to an end. Heavy rains swelled creeks

Chimney Rock in Nebraska was a major landmark on the Mormons' westward journey.

that the companies needed to cross and turned the wagon trail to mud. Poisonous rattlesnakes slithered out from behind rocks or shrubs. Babies were born, and people died from illness, disease, gunshot wounds, and wagon accidents. When someone died, the survivors had little time to mourn. They placed the bodies in quickly dug graves and moved on.

As the long wagon train made its way west, Biddy tended sheep that were being taken to Utah. It is possible that she was also called upon to act as a midwife or nurse, helping with births and illnesses occurring along the trail. But her main task was to care for the sheep, a job she was well-equipped to handle.

Biddy was "a woman of almost masculine strength" who "trudged patiently behind," according to a 1909 newspaper article that recalled the lives of prominent women in Los Angeles history. Of course, she also had to watch over her own family. Her daughter Harriet was just an infant. Her oldest girl, Ellen, was about 9 years old at the time, and Ann was about 4.

This was no ordinary journey for Biddy, her children, or the others who had spent their lives in the South or the East. They traveled through a land that often seemed foreign, and the sights and sounds of the West amazed them. They had never before seen anything like the large herds of buffalo that grazed on the Western plains and that many of the men hunted. Nor had they seen anything like the rocky landscape, which one 1848 traveler described in his journal as "remarkable, interesting, and romantic."

Biddy's company also encountered Native Americans, especially the Sioux, who followed buffalo herds across the Western plains. The pioneer trains also met members from the Pawnee and Shoshone tribes.

A group of Mormons travel up a trail through the Rocky Mountains.

The encounters were usually pleasant, and Mormon Trail diaries tell of friendly trading that often went on between the pioneers and the Native Americans whose land they traveled through. The pioneers and Indians also exchanged culture, sometimes playing music and dancing for each other when the Mormons camped alongside an Indian settlement.

The last 100 miles (160 km) to Salt Lake City were the most difficult for the travelers. The elevation of the land was much higher than before, and an epidemic called mountain fever struck many people. The mountains were hard to climb with heavy wagons, and there was less grass for the animals to eat.

Biddy's family and the Smiths were among the last people in the expedition to finish the journey. They reached Salt Lake City in mid-October. The trip had been exhausting, but their difficulties were not over. While some of the Mississippi Mormons had sent their slaves ahead to Utah to build cabins, Smith still had no place for his party to live. He had to scramble to get some type of housing built before the harsh winter in the mountains set in.

The entire Smith household spent the next two and a half years in Utah. The Smiths were among thousands of Mormons who helped turn Salt Lake City into an oasis in the desert. Biddy, Hannah, and their children joined a growing number of black

Mormon travelers arrive at the Great Salt Lake.

Utah residents. Some were free blacks who became Mormon converts, but most of them were slaves who came with their Mormon owners.

It was a difficult life for both white and black pioneers in Utah. With few trees in the area, the desertlike environment posed challenges for farming and building, but the mountain snows did provide a good source of water.

Westward growth threw off a delicate balance in Washington, D.C. By 1850, the population of Northern states had increased, with many immigrants settling in large cities such as New York, Philadelphia, and Boston. In the U.S. House of Representatives, congressmen from Northern states outnumbered those of Southern states. But the Senate, where each state sent two senators, was evenly divided between Northern and Southern lawmakers. There were 15 free states and 15 slave states. Southern lawmakers hoped to expand the number of slave states, while Northern lawmakers hoped to prevent that.

Mormon men were often called away by the church on missionary trips to win new converts in other parts of the country or in other lands. The wives and children they left behind had to keep their new homesteads going. In the early Utah days, church leaders also directed some members to go on trips, change careers, or move to new areas, all in the name of following God's call.

Robert Smith was chosen to go with a group to explore southern Utah. Managing the household alone was difficult for Rebecca, who had just given birth to a baby. At least she had Biddy and Hannah to rely on when Smith left on his mission.

The Mormons welcomed black converts into their ranks, but the church did not act to improve the situation of people being held in slavery. In fact, the church simply did not try to change anyone's ideas on slavery. The Mormons made no laws in Utah for or against it. A church leader named Orson Hyde wrote in a Mormon newspaper in 1851:

> *[W]e do not wish to oppose the laws of the country. If there is sin in selling a slave, let the individual who sells him bear that sin, and not the Church.*

Although Biddy was a religious woman, she did not join the Mormon faith. Still, the church would have a major impact on her life. Smith still had his eye on California as the family's final destination. He wanted to be part of a Mormon expedition to Southern California.

As a new state, California had been part of a fierce battle in Washington, D.C., over the legality of slavery in America's new Western territories. A compromise in Congress made California a free state. Traveling there would not instantly make Biddy free, but it would give her the chance she needed to break away from slavery. ❧

5 CALIFORNIA DREAMS

Chapter

❦

As Biddy and the rest of Robert Smith's household had been making their way to Utah in 1848, an important discovery occurred in California. This discovery would not only change American history but would spark a series of events that would allow Biddy to seize control of her own destiny.

California was already considered a great prize when it was won from Mexico in the Mexican War. The fighting had ended in 1847, and the United States took control of California and other territories in the Southwest. California held lush farmland, plentiful grazing areas, abundant minerals, beautiful scenery, and an ideal climate. Then gold was discovered in central California near the city of Sacramento in January 1848. As the thought of

The West Coast was seen as the land of opportunity by many Americans. But getting there from the East was a challenge before the transcontinental railroad was completed in 1869. Cross-country travel meant going through territory of Native Americans who feared losing their lands, over mountains with deadly winter storms, and through harsh deserts with no water for miles. Another way to get to California or the Oregon Territory was by boat—all the way around the tip of South America and then back up the western coasts of South, Central, and North America, a journey that could take months.

instant riches spread, people stampeded to California from all over the United States, Europe, and even Australia and Asia.

Before California was even established as a state, people began to flock there in search of gold. Local leaders were forced to take steps to deal with the lawlessness that came with the flood of gold miners.

Just before the 1848 gold discovery, about 6,000 white settlers lived in California. By the end of 1849, more than 20,000 people— many of them white Americans— lived in the city of San Francisco alone. That same year, the people of California approved a state constitution forbidding slavery. In 1850, California was admitted to the United States as a free state.

Biddy's owner may not have realized that California was a free state, or he may not have understood what that could mean for his household. Robert Smith had his hopes set on going to California, but he and his family would have

to stay in Utah for a while.

Meanwhile, the Mormon settlement at the Great Salt Lake became a busy stopping place for people heading west in search of gold. California fever, as the gold rush was called, also infected some Mormons, and some of them followed the westward rush. But Mormons who decided to stay in Utah and sell supplies to travelers made more money than the average gold miner.

California's farmland sounded attractive to Smith, who still wanted to live as a farmer and rancher. In 1851, he volunteered to join an expedition to establish a Mormon settlement in the southern part of the state. The trip to California was

Biddy Mason was born a slave in rural Georgia. Once freed, she lived out her days in Los Angeles, California.

The trail from Salt Lake City to California led travelers through miles of hot, dry, and rugged desert.

another long, difficult journey. The wagon train was made up of 150 wagons and a group that included Smith's family and slaves. Biddy again traveled on foot, taking care of the livestock behind the wagons.

The Mormon group spent the spring of 1851 traveling to California. Like the last leg of their Salt Lake City journey in 1848, it was the last part of the trip to California, trudging through the Mojave Desert, that was the most difficult. Biddy endured long days in the sun, often without enough water to drink. She had to watch over animals, who struggled and sometimes stumbled in the sand. She often had to help free carts and wagons that had gotten stuck.

In early June, Biddy and the rest of the Smith party arrived safely in San Bernardino in Southern California. Many other newcomers were still pouring in at the time. Whether they came from Ohio or Australia, the newly arrived Californians had been lured by the opportunity for a fresh start in life and perhaps even riches. The dark side of this population growth was the fact that white settlers often took property with little regard for the previous occupants—the Mexicans and Indians who had long made the West their home.

It wasn't long before some Mormon leaders bought a large section of land from a family that had received the land as a grant from the Mexican government. The church members decided to build a cluster of homes on the shared property, which was in the San Bernardino area. But Smith decided to move away from the group. He claimed some property not yet settled by whites along the Santa Ana River, near a small but growing town called Los Angeles. Smith would soon fulfill his lifelong dream of owning good farmland.

Smith established a cattle ranch on the land with the livestock he had brought along from Utah. He

Mormons settled in California's San Bernardino Valley.

also purchased more animals in Los Angeles to expand his herd. Over the next few years, Smith built up a prosperous ranch with the help of his slaves, including Biddy and her daughters.

The population of Los Angeles in the early 1850s was about 1,600, and some accounts put the number of free blacks there at fewer than 20. Biddy and her daughters were fortunate to make friends with some of the free blacks in Los Angeles. They likely told Biddy that her status as a slave was illegal in California. Freedom seemed to be within Biddy's reach. Even though state law prohibited slavery, it was not that easy for people like Biddy to be declared free.

The legal position of slaves was a complicated issue in California at the time. The law was unclear about the standing of slaves who were brought into the state by their owners. Some owners granted freedom to their slaves but kept them as indentured, or unpaid, servants. Slave owners also discovered that local authorities didn't bother them much about owning slaves. If they were brought to court on the issue, they usually ended up winning and being allowed to keep their slaves.

The fate of escaped slaves and free blacks was also an issue in California. These people were at risk nationwide because of the Fugitive Slave Act. The law, which had been passed in 1850, stirred outrage among many people in the North. Slaves who escaped by the Underground Railroad and other means had found safety there for years. Now Canada became the only place where escaped slaves could truly be safe.

Even free blacks who had lived their entire lives in the North felt threatened under the Fugitive Slave Act. They heard about free blacks who were mistaken for escaped slaves, taken from their Northern homes, and sent to live in slavery in the South. They feared it could happen to them, too.

By the mid-1850s, in the midst of the slavery

CAUTION!!

COLORED PEOPLE

OF BOSTON, ONE & ALL,

You are hereby respectfully CAUTIONED and advised, to avoid conversing with the

Watchmen and Police Officers of Boston,

For since the recent ORDER OF THE MAYOR & ALDERMEN, they are empowered to act as

KIDNAPPERS

AND

Slave Catchers,

And they have already been actually employed in KIDNAPPING, CATCHING, AND KEEPING SLAVES. Therefore, if you value your LIBERTY, and the *Welfare of the Fugitives* among you, *Shun* them in every possible manner, as so many *HOUNDS* on the track of the most unfortunate of your race.

Keep a Sharp Look Out for KIDNAPPERS, and have TOP EYE open.

APRIL 24, 1851.

The Fugitive Slave Act put escaped slaves at risk even in free states.

controversy, Smith's hopes for his farm and ranch soured. He became involved in a land dispute with California Mormon leaders, who by the summer of 1855 had decided they wanted Smith's property. Plans were to parcel the land out among other Mormons, but Smith did not happily cooperate. In fact, he split with the Mormon church over its plans, and he began to consider uprooting his family and his slaves once again.

Smith had another reason to leave California. A state law passed in 1852 said that people who brought slaves to California before statehood could keep those slaves if they left the state. It isn't clear when Smith found out about this law or whether Biddy and the other slaves understood what it meant for them. But once Smith realized the significance of the law and after his disagreements with Mormon leaders, he decided to head for Texas.

Late in 1855, Smith began making plans to move his household, including Biddy, Hannah, and their 10 children. Hannah was pregnant with her eighth child. Once they left California, there would be no chance for freedom for Biddy and the other slaves. Texas law allowed slavery. ℀

Chapter
6 A LEGAL
CHALLENGE

❧⟨✕⟩❧

Late in December 1855, Biddy and the rest of the Smith household left their comfortable ranch and set up camp in the Santa Monica hills, where they prepared to leave for Texas. About 25 people made up the group—the Smiths and their children, the slave families, and some young men hired to help with the journey.

Smith's decision to leave his home and camp nearby seemed suspicious. The December nights would have been cold and uncomfortable for all, with the women and children sleeping in wagons and most of the men sleeping under the stars.

He most likely had one simple reason for setting up camp: He wanted to isolate his slaves to keep them from learning more about California's

Robert Smith hoped to isolate his slaves at a campsite in the hills outside Los Angeles.

antislavery laws. With that in mind, Smith took his slaves to a quiet camp in the hills as he got ready to move. He planned to leave California by New Year's Day, 1856.

One night, a group of men led by two county sheriffs from Los Angeles and San Bernardino counties rode on horseback into Smith's campsite. The lawmen showed Smith a legal document that allowed them to take Biddy and the rest of Smith's slaves to Los Angeles. The legal order would keep the slaves in California, at least until a court hearing could take place. Smith had no choice but to abide by the sheriffs' demands.

The document the sheriffs carried was a petition of habeas corpus. The name is a Latin legal term meaning "you have the body." It is used when a court must decide whether someone is being held without good cause. In Biddy's case, a judge would have to hear the facts and decide her fate.

Habeas corpus, the legal move that kept Robert Smith from taking Biddy and his other slaves to Texas, dated back to the 1600s in England. It represented an important right that is still protected by the U.S. Constitution. This right prevents a person from being unjustly jailed or held under someone else's authority.

Usually, a petition of habeas corpus is used in cases involving a person being held in jail. It requires the jailed person to be brought before the court and forces authorities holding that person to justify their actions. A judge can then decide if the person is being held fairly or if the person should be set free.

Biddy's case was slightly different. Since slavery was illegal in California, a petition of habeas corpus allowed Biddy to be taken from Smith until her status could be decided for certain.

The lawmen removed the slaves from Smith's

camp and took them to the Los Angeles jail. They were locked up, but they were not under arrest. The local judge wanted to protect the slaves, to keep them from going back to Smith or from being taken back against their will. Jail, the judge concluded, seemed to be the safest place.

Ironically, Biddy, Hannah, and their children would have to stay in jail to win their freedom. It was a strange twist, but the slaves had no other choice.

A bit of mystery also surrounded the last-minute rescue of these Texas-bound slaves. Someone had to alert the judge to the slaves' situation. Someone also had to convince the judge that a writ of habeas corpus was necessary. Records from the era do not say for certain who spoke up on the slaves' behalf.

However, two young men seem likely to have been involved. The free black men, Charles Owens and Manuel Pepper, had good reason to want the slaves to be free and stay in California. They were in love with two of the young slaves— Charles with Biddy's 17-year-old daughter, Ellen, and

> *Judge Benjamin Hayes studied law at St. Mary's College in Baltimore, Maryland. He was just 24 years old when he completed his law degree. He then moved west to Missouri, where he practiced law in the city of Independence, beginning in the early 1840s. He traveled to California in 1849, where he helped create courts and legal offices in a small community called Los Angeles.*

The Los Angeles jail sat on a hillside near the intersection of Main, Spring, and Temple streets.

Manuel with Hannah's 17-year-old daughter, Ann. Charles knew about Smith's plan to take the slaves to Texas. Biddy had told him about it and shared her fears with him.

It is also possible the writ of habeas corpus was requested by Charles' father, Robert Owens. The elder Owens was an early black pioneer in Southern California who ran a corral in Los Angeles. He and his wife, Winnie, were successful residents of the city when it had just a handful of black citizens. They had become friends with Biddy and her family.

Biddy's friend Robert Owens had his own interesting story. In 1930, Owens' grandson recorded details of his grandfather's life. "In the year 1850 my grand-father arrived in L.A., crossing the plains by ox team in six months," he wrote. Robert Owens made many friends in California, including a future gov-ernor, John Downey, and a doctor who would later hire Biddy. Owens "was a trader principally in horses and mules. He made many trips to the large ranches in San Diego and returned with two & three hundred ani-mals." Owens built a successful business and became a wealthy property owner.

Judge Benjamin Hayes, a Maryland native who came to California in 1849, would hear the case. Perhaps Smith expected sympathy from Hayes, since Maryland was a slave state. But Hayes took the issue of freedom for Biddy and the other slaves seriously. He first heard about the case when two people visited his home in late December 1855. Court documents do not name the two. The visitors pushed for the writ of habeas corpus, and the judge granted their request.

Hayes felt sorry about keep-ing Biddy, Hannah, and their chil-dren in the city jail. He worried that it might even frighten them enough to make them want to return to Smith, who had gone back to his ranch. But the slaves willingly slept on cots in the jail cells and spent their days under the watch of a deputy, who later testified in court about how the slaves were afraid of their owner.

On New Year's Day, 1856, Judge Hayes called

Smith to his chambers to get the slave owner's point of view. Smith claimed that Biddy and Hannah had traveled across the country with his family by "their own consent," as Hayes later wrote. Smith said he wasn't holding them as slaves but caring for them as family members. Smith also pointed out that the case was started not by Biddy or Hannah but by others. He claimed the legal challenge was the work of meddling outsiders, and there was no proof the slaves were unhappy living with his family.

Nevertheless, the judge determined that the issues of slavery and freedom were important enough to demand a full hearing in court. ᦡ

Chapter
7 THE CASE FOR FREEDOM

❧❦❧

The court hearing to decide the fate of Biddy, Hannah, and their children finally began in mid-January 1856. The nation's conflict over slavery was becoming more intense. The old balance between slave states in the South and free states in the North was gone. The growth of settlement in the West and the push to admit new states stirred conflict between those who wanted to end slavery and those who wanted to expand it.

Lawmakers in Washington, D.C., had struggled for decades to satisfy both sides in the fight. Back in 1820, the U.S. Congress had passed a law known as the Missouri Compromise. The agreement allowed Missouri to join the country as a slave state but barred slavery in a huge area north and west of Missouri.

A Los Angeles monument to Biddy Mason includes some of the judge's words about her case.

In 1850, a group of new laws allowed California to join the country as a free state. The issue of slavery was left undecided in a broad section of the Southwest, where Arizona, New Mexico, Utah, and Nevada are today.

Then in 1854, Congress voted to let the issue of slavery in the West be decided by citizens of the new states. As a result, settlers for and against slavery rushed to Nebraska and Kansas. Conflicts broke out between the settlers, and the results were sometimes deadly.

At the same time, a Missouri court was considering an important case. A slave named Dred Scott had sued for his freedom, and his story had a lot in common with Biddy's. Scott's owner took him to live in the free North, where Scott stayed for years and even got married. Later, Scott's owner took him to Missouri, which was a slave state. Scott filed a suit in a Missouri court on the grounds that his years in the North gave him legal

Dred Scott hoped the court would grant him freedom.

standing as a free citizen. In 1850, a circuit court in St. Louis, Missouri, ruled that Scott was free, but the Missouri Supreme Court reversed that decision two years later. Scott's case then moved to the federal courts. Eventually, the U.S. Supreme Court would decide his fate.

Roger Taney, chief justice of the U.S. Supreme Court, considers the Dred Scott case.

In 1857, the Supreme Court issued a devastating ruling for all African-Americans. The court said that

because Scott was black, he could not sue and was not even a citizen. The ruling also threw out the Missouri Compromise and opened new territory to slavery. The Supreme Court's action caused outrage in the North and put the nation on the path that led to the Civil War.

Biddy's case went to court before the Scott matter was decided. She was fortunate, because the Scott ruling would have left her with no hope for freedom. With Scott's case still unresolved, Biddy's situation in Los Angeles attracted a lot of attention.

Crowds filled the courtroom, and others followed the case in the newspapers. Judge Hayes believed that many in California did not want the court involved in affairs between Smith and his slaves. The judge later wrote, "with 'public opinion' against me, I tried the case."

While it concerned all of Smith's slaves, the hearing centered on Biddy. However, Biddy could not take the stand to explain her wishes. She couldn't say what she knew about Texas and what Smith had promised. She couldn't testify at all. California law prevented it. The law said that a nonwhite person could not testify in court against a white person.

Biddy's hopes for freedom seemed to be in serious trouble on the trial's second day. Her lawyer did not show up in court. Robert Smith's lawyer, Alonzo Thomas, promptly called for the case to be dismissed. After all, he claimed, Biddy's lawyer was nowhere to be found. Right then, Smith may have thought he had won his battle to keep his slaves.

Dred Scott briefly experienced life as a free man. After years of trying to win his freedom, Scott suffered a serious setback when the U.S. Supreme court ruled in 1857 that he was not a citizen and had no right to sue. The decision was a blow to all slaves and to people who wanted to abolish slavery. But the sons of Scott's former master came to his aid after the ruling. He purchased Scott and his wife, Harriet, from their current owner and set them free. Unfortunately, Dred Scott died less than a year later.

But the judge had some questions about the case. Hayes asked Biddy if she had told her lawyer that she no longer needed him. He asked if she had spoken with him at all since they had been in court the day before.

Biddy seemed as surprised as anyone that her attorney had quit in the middle of the case. Although Smith's lawyer denied it, Hayes grew suspicious that Smith had paid Biddy's lawyer to quit the trial, perhaps even threatened him.

Hayes also wondered if the slaves understood that they were sacrificing a chance for freedom by returning to Texas. He worried that Smith, who was struggling financially at the time, intended to make money by selling his slaves when he reached Texas.

The judge ignored Thomas' suggestion that he dismiss Biddy's case. Although she wasn't allowed to testify in court, Biddy was about to get her chance to speak. Hayes got around the law by interviewing Biddy and Hannah's daughter Ann, in his chambers.

Two Los Angeles citizens were present as witnesses.

At last, Biddy told how she was worried about moving to Texas: "I have always done what I have

Judge Benjamin Hayes in a picture taken nearly 20 years after he handled Biddy's case

69

been told to do," she told Hayes. However, she said:

*I always feared this trip to Texas, since I
first heard of it. Mr. Smith told me I would
be just as free in Texas as here.*

The judge could not interview Hannah, who was away caring for a newborn son. But Hayes discovered that Ann was also concerned about moving to Texas. Ann asked the judge, "Will I be as free as here?"

The judge's decision was further complicated by a California law meant to protect African-American children. The law said no black child could be moved to a state where he or she would be enslaved. So even if Biddy and Hannah wanted to stay with the Smiths, Judge Hayes would be forced to make their children stay in California.

When the judge told Biddy about the law, she was even more determined to stay in California. "I do not wish to be separated from my children, and do not in such a case wish to go," she said.

Judge Benjamin Hayes had been a slave owner before he traveled to California. Hayes met Emily Chauncey in Missouri, and they married there in 1848. When Emily's father died, he left at least two slaves to Emily and her new husband. But Hayes did not live as a slaveholder for long. He and Emily had been married less than a year when he left for California. He planned to send for his wife later, which he did after he became county attorney in Los Angeles in 1850. When Emily left Missouri in 1851, she went without slaves.

Sept. 20th 1863 –

To F. Hinton (Fort Yuma)

"An interesting reminiscence occurs to me at the moment. In the year 1854, at Los Angeles, with "public opinion" against me, I tried the case of fourteen negroes, claiming the protection of the writ of Habeas Corpus. I discharged them, as entitled to freedom. I was denounced as — an abolitionist! For declaring a simple proposition of law — for granting a clear constitutional right! Even at Sacramento, I was 'damned' (so Gov. Downey informed me.) A month passed: one day my little boy from a buggy, under the heels of the horse; one of these same poor negro women, whom Providence placed nearby, rushed under the

In this 1863 letter to a friend, Judge Hayes explained his feelings about the Biddy Mason case.

When Hayes finished talking with the slaves, he announced he would make his decision the following day. The next morning, on January 19, 1856,

Hayes read his decision aloud to a full courtroom.

Hayes had grown up around slavery in Maryland. He knew that some slave owners tried harder than others to treat their slaves well. But in his decision, he stated:

> [E]ven without a bad intention, a man is not permitted to do a positive injury to others, when it can be prevented.

In other words, sometimes people do wrong things to other people without meaning to. But even so, it should not be allowed to happen. It was possible, Hayes said, that Smith didn't plan to harm Biddy and the other slaves and truly considered them family. But, the judge said, taking them from California to a slave state like Texas could harm them.

In fact, Hayes questioned Smith's intentions, accusing him of "persuading and enticing and seducing" the slaves to leave California with the "false promise held out to them that they will be as free in the state of Texas as in the state of California."

In his decision, Hayes noted that none of the slaves could read or write, and they were perhaps unclear of their rights in California. He also thought they might be under duress, or pressure, from Smith. The judge added that the slaves did not have "free will so as to give their binding consent" or to make an informed decision about going to Texas.

Most important, the judge declared:

> *[Since] all of the said persons of color are entitled to their freedom, and are free and cannot be held in slavery or involuntary servitude, it is therefore argued that they are entitled to their freedom and are free forever.*

He added, "Their liberty will be greatly jeopardized" with a move to Texas and "there is good reason to ... believe that they may be sold into slavery."

Biddy, her children, and Smith's other slaves were now no longer slaves. They were no longer the property of another person, and they were free to stay in California.

Judge Hayes wanted to make sure Hannah also knew about his decision. He ordered that she be brought to the courtroom the following Monday. On that morning, though, she did not show up, and neither did Smith.

Some people may have feared the Smiths had already left for Texas, taking Hannah with them. The sheriff rode off to the

After Biddy was freed, Judge Hayes' son was involved in an accident. The boy, who was about 3 years old at the time, fell from a buggy and landed at the feet of a horse. A passerby scooped up the child before any harm could come to him. That passerby, Hayes later reported in a letter to a friend, was one of the former slaves the judge had freed about a month earlier.

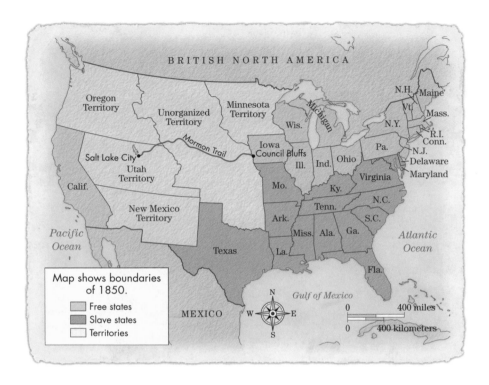

BRITISH NORTH AMERICA

Oregon Territory

Unorganized Territory

Minnesota Territory

Michigan

Wis.

N.H. Maine

Vt.

Mass.

N.Y.

R.I.
Conn.

Mormon Trail

Salt Lake City

Utah Territory

Calif.

Iowa
Council Bluffs

Ill. Ind. Ohio

Pa.

N.J.

Delaware

Maryland

Virginia

Mo.

Ky.

New Mexico Territory

Tenn.

N.C.

Ark.

S.C.

Pacific
Ocean

Miss. Ala. Ga.

Texas

La.

Atlantic
Ocean

Fla.

Map shows boundaries of 1850.

Free states

Slave states

Territories

MEXICO

N

Gulf of Mexico

W E

S

0   400 miles

0   400 kilometers

California was a new state in 1850, and settlers had begun to flow into Western lands long held by Native Americans and Mexicans.

Smith ranch, where Hannah had returned to give birth to a son. Hannah and the Smiths were still at the ranch, which was a relief to Hannah's loved ones.

Hannah had mixed emotions about Hayes' decision. She had grown up with Rebecca in South Carolina and had lived with Rebecca and Robert Smith for many years. Hannah also had eight children and a grandchild. She faced the difficult question of whether she would be able to take care of them all on her own without the help of the Smiths.

Her future would be uncertain and challenging. But she chose to stay in California with her children and experience her newfound freedom.

Biddy had been a slave for 37 years. For all those years, she had known only the forced labor and a long, difficult trip across the continent. Now Biddy was finally free. Her legal battle had taken less than one month.

She was fortunate to have friends who helped and encouraged her along the way. She was also fortunate to have a judge who was committed to California's antislavery law.

In another decade, all slaves in the United States would be free. The end of the Civil War in 1865 would give all slaves the freedom that Biddy now enjoyed. In the next 10 years, Biddy would also be successful at many things that would have been impossible if she had gone to Texas. In fact, Biddy would make a life for herself that probably was beyond the imagination of anyone still trapped in slavery.

African-American women throughout the West created their own social clubs and organizations. Many of the clubs focused on community service or learning about culture. One group of African-American women in Los Angeles called themselves the Book Lovers Club. The wife of Biddy Mason's grandson, Robert C. Owens, performed for groups such as the Women's Monday Afternoon Club of Covina (California). She was a popular singer in Los Angeles at the time.

8 STARTING OVER

❧᷂❧

In explanation of his decision to release Biddy, Hannah, and their children from slavery, Judge Benjamin Hayes declared the adult women free to "become settled and go to work for themselves—in peace and without fear." For the first time in her life, Biddy could "go to work" for herself.

This privilege also meant challenges. She would need to find work and earn enough to feed and house her family. Biddy got some help right away from her friends Robert and Winnie Owens. They invited Biddy and her daughters to stay at their home while they got started in life as free citizens. The October 1856 marriage of Biddy's daughter Ellen to Charles Owens made a lasting bond between the families.

The only known photograph of Biddy Mason, who was in her 50s when it was taken

A mural showing Biddy at work with Dr. John Strother Griffin

Biddy was fortunate to be an experienced nurse and midwife. She had skills that allowed her to be paid more than other newly freed blacks. Biddy soon started working as the assistant to Dr. John Strother Griffin. The doctor was Judge Hayes' brother-in-law and was also acquainted with the Owens family.

Griffin kept Biddy busy. He ran a private practice, served as the doctor at the county hospital, and cared for prisoners at the Los Angeles jail. Biddy assisted him in all his work. He paid her $2.50 per day, a good wage at that time. Biddy also worked on her own, serving as a midwife for many new mothers. Sometimes her patients had little money and couldn't afford to pay her, so Biddy accepted "in kind" payments such as vegetables, eggs, or other goods.

As a midwife, she learned to use herbal remedies to help pregnant women who were about to give birth. She would also teach women exercises that would make labor, or the birthing process, easier. After a baby was born, Biddy would often stay with the family to cook meals and care for the other children while the mother rested with her new baby.

Her skills as a midwife were in great demand in the Los Angeles area. She delivered hundreds of babies from the time she began practicing in 1856. As a nurse and midwife, she met all kinds of families in Los Angeles. She made rounds throughout the growing city, traveling with her nursing bag to tiny shacks and also to more comfortable homes where she helped deliver babies.

Biddy's family grew, as well. Her daughter Ellen and her husband Charles welcomed two sons into the world. The oldest was named Robert C. Owens, after his grandfather, and their younger son was named Henry. In 1860, the U.S. Census, the official counting of residents in all the states, reported that a woman named Bridget lived with Ellen and Charles Owens. The census showed that another local black family listed a 12-year-old girl named Harriet Mason living with them. It was quite possible that Biddy's daughter Harriet was earning money as a live-in servant.

Around 1860, Biddy began using Mason as her last name. Los Angeles records do not clearly explain how or why she chose the name. Some accounts suggest it was in honor of Amasa Mason Lyman, one of the Mormon guides on the trip to California.

A Los Angeles memorial to Biddy shows the tools she used as a midwife.

Others suggest that Mason was the name of the Georgia family that owned Biddy at birth.

Prisoners at the jail soon came to know her as a friend. She visited them often, "speaking a word of cheer and leaving some token and a prayerful hope with every prisoner," according to a newspaper article recalling Biddy's life. She was well-known in the slums of Los Angeles and was called Grandma Mason for her kind treatment of the city's neediest citizens. Well-respected older women such as Biddy often were called Aunt or Grandma.

Outbreaks of the deadly disease smallpox were not unusual in the area, and Biddy bravely went to nurse those who needed care, although there was always a chance she could catch the disease and die. Sadly, she was not able to save her own daughter Ann, who died in August 1857, possibly of smallpox.

Many people needed Biddy's nursing services, and she enjoyed a good reputation among the townspeople. They would see her at all times of day and night on the streets of Los Angeles. She carried a large black bag that held her midwife supplies. On her way, she might stop to tell a friend or neighbor that she was on her way to "catch" a baby, the casual term used for delivering a newborn.

Mason also had to carry another important item with her at all times. It was a copy of Judge Hayes' ruling that declared her free. She wanted to make

After the 1856 trial in Los Angeles, Hannah and Biddy went their separate ways. Hannah returned to San Bernardino, where she had lived with the Smith family. Like Biddy, Hannah became a midwife. Sometimes she was referred to as Hannah Smith, no doubt because she had belonged to the Smith family for so many years. Hannah's name isn't mentioned in any local records from Southern California after 1868, when she was 44 years old. If she had died, a death certificate would have been filed. It is likely she moved away from California.

sure she had proof of her freedom, since the Fugitive Slave Act was still in effect. She most likely had heard about free blacks who were mistaken for escaped slaves, seized on the street, and shipped off to a slave state. She always wanted to be able to prove her identity and her right to be free.

As Mason began her life of freedom in California, her former owners journeyed on to Texas, as planned. The Smith family left California in March 1856. Their trip through the deserts of Arizona and New Mexico was dangerous at times. Robert's hired hands plotted against him, and the family had close calls along the trail with members of the Comanche tribe of Native Americans. But all of the travelers arrived in Texas safely and settled near San Antonio in June 1856. Rebecca's family again gave the Smiths some slaves—a woman and her young son—who remained with the Smiths as servants even after the Civil War ended in 1865.

Biddy's family stayed at the home of Robert Owens after they were freed.

The Smiths' sons fought for the Southern Confederate Army in the Civil War, and the two older sons later lived colorful lives as cowboys in the West. Robert and Rebecca Smith spent the rest of their lives in Texas. Robert died in 1891 at the age of 86, and Rebecca died in 1899 at the age of 89. ❧

SHARING THE FRUITS OF HER LABORS

Chapter 9

Biddy Mason's case had a lasting effect on many people in California, including the judge who set her free. Judge Benjamin Hayes made some enemies by freeing the Smiths' slaves, but he was reelected as district judge in 1858. Later, Hayes wrote about the African-American community in Los Angeles:

> In the Spring of 1850, probably three or four colored persons were in this city. In 1875 they number about one hundred and seventy five souls; many of whom hold good city property, acquired through their industry.

Of course, Mason was among those people who were doing well in Los Angeles.

Mason's property on Spring Street became part of a thriving area in Los Angeles.

Mason continued to earn a good living as a nurse and midwife, but she was careful to spend her money wisely. She believed it was important to save some of her hard-earned dollars. After 10 years, she had finally saved up enough money to buy a piece of property. She was the first black woman to own land in Los Angeles.

In 1866, Biddy bought some property on Spring Street for $250. At first, her land was on the edge of town. A map of that area from around 1870 shows just a few buildings on each block along Spring Street, with plenty of open space.

But Spring Street grew into a popular area for industry and businesses, and Biddy's property increased greatly in value. Even so, she told her children she never wanted them to sell her homestead, the land where she owned her first home.

The property was a symbol of her hopes and dreams to give her family a better life. Mason noticed how many immigrants came to Los Angeles, did backbreaking work, and lived on very little money. She saw Chinese and Mexican people working in fruit orchards, Native Americans tending grapes in vineyards, and Japanese working in flower beds, all for a meager wage. After a lifetime of hard labor herself, Mason wanted a better life for her children and grandchildren. She continued to buy other pieces of land when she could afford them.

Mason's first house on Spring Street in Los Angeles

Mason lived in the small, wood-framed house on the Spring Street property for many years. In 1884, she sold part of the property and built a brick building on the part she kept. By then, Spring Street was a booming business area with shops, restaurants, and boardinghouses lining the street.

Mason rented the first floor of her new building to businesses and lived in an apartment on the second floor. The portion of the property she sold went for $1,500, which was six times the amount she had paid for all of her land there. Her other land purchases were also paying off. In 1868, Mason paid $375 for a lot on Olive Street, and in 1884, she sold it for $2,800.

A class portrait at the Spring Street School, located near the first property purchased by Mason

Although she had no formal education and still could not read or write, Mason was a wise business-woman and profited from her real estate invest-ments. She also continued her work as a nurse and midwife.

She had become a relatively wealthy person, but she didn't use her money to buy fancy clothes or a lavish home. Instead, she became a philanthropist, who shared her profits with her neighbors.

Los Angeles was sometimes flooded by seasonal rains, and the high waters forced people out of their homes and destroyed their possessions. Not long after she sold her Olive Street property in 1884, Mason told a neighborhood grocer to give food to the people who had lost their homes in the floods. She would pay the bill. Biddy became known for her generosity, and it wasn't long before people came to her home asking for help.

Drawing on her strong faith in God, Mason found yet another way to help her community. In 1872, a group of African-Americans met at her home and decided to organize a church. Mason's pioneering spirit and generosity was crucial in creating the Los Angeles First African Methodist Episcopal Church (F.A.M.E.), the first African-American church in the city.

The church began in Mason's home. Although it struggled at first, the congregation soon moved to its own location. In lean times, Mason helped the young congregation by paying the minister's salary and the taxes on the property.

The church building was shared with the Los Angeles Board of Education. The board used the building as the city's first public school for black children. In the late 1800s, leaders from F.A.M.E. fought to end segregation in all of the city's public

schools, so black and white children could attend school together.

In 1885, Mason helped her grandsons open a livery stable on her property. People who didn't have their own stables paid to keep their horses there. When the livery became a success, she rewarded her grandsons by giving them some of her property. The land was not completely free, however. Mason required "the sum of love and affection and ten dollars," as the deed said.

As Mason grew older, her failing health made it difficult to continue her good works in the neighborhood. People were still lining up at her gate to see her, but finally, one of her grandsons had to tell them she wasn't able to come out.

On January 15, 1891, at the age of 72, Biddy Mason died. The Fort Street Methodist Episcopal Church, where she had attended services for many years, held a simple funeral in her honor. She was buried in the Evergreen Cemetery in Los Angeles. Nearly a century later, in 1988, the church she helped found, F.A.M.E., put a headstone at her gravesite. The stone had the dates of her birth and death and listed the many ways she would be remembered:

> *Former Slave*
> *Philanthropist*
> *Humanitarian*
> *Founding Member*
> *First African Methodist*
> *Episcopal Church*
> *1872*
> *Los Angeles, California*

By the time Biddy Mason died, her Spring Street home was in the middle of a bustling business area, full of shops and businesses in buildings several stories high. As the city grew around Mason's property, her personal wealth grew with it. In the end, she had built a sizable fortune. Several years after her death, Mason's estate was valued at about $300,000, which would be at least $6 million today.

The area where Mason once lived is now considered an old neighborhood. Her home on Spring Street is gone. Los Angeles has changed greatly from the dusty little town Mason saw in 1851 when she first arrived in California. But visitors to her old neighborhood can still get an idea of what her life was like in the 1800s, thanks to some public art projects dedicated to her extraordinary life story.

One of the artworks—presented on Biddy Mason Day in Los Angeles on November 16, 1989—is a sculpture titled *Biddy Mason: Time and Place*. It's an 80-foot-long (24-meter) stone wall designed by Sheila Levrant de Bretteville that stands outside the Broadway Spring Center. All along the wall are images and words that help describe who Mason was and what she accomplished in life.

Another large piece of art, *House of the Open Hand*, designed by Betye Saar, is displayed inside the Broadway Spring Center. It features two walls that come together in an L shape that is meant to resemble Mason's house from the outside. The piece features a large image of Mason on her front porch

Today, the Los Angeles First African Methodist Episcopal church, or F.A.M.E., has 18,000 members, employs 180 people, and has 2,000 volunteers who help run community programs in Los Angeles. F.A.M.E.'s home is now a modern building about 10 miles (16 km) south of where the original church stood in the 1800s.

F.A.M.E. church occupied a few locations in Los Angeles before its current home on Harvard Boulevard was built in the 1960s.

with her Owens family friends.

Mason provided for her family even after her death. She left her children and grandchildren her savings and her valuable property. Thanks to Mason's hard work and humble life, her grandsons enjoyed opportunities that many Americans could only dream of. In 1905, a *Los Angeles Times* story about Mason's grandson Robert C. Owens called him the "Richest Negro in Los Angeles."

Biddy's daughters, Ellen and Harriet, appeared in court several times to settle various disagreements between them. Ellen, who remarried after Charles Owens died in 1882, controlled the estate her mother left behind, which is perhaps the reason she and Harriet ended up in court.

Because Mason lived simply and never learned to read and write, she didn't leave behind any

A visitor to the monument honoring Mason looks over an image of a deed for land she purchased.

letters or journals that would give us a glimpse of what her daily life was really like. But one important thing that Mason once said did survive over the years. Her descendants and others who admire her life and accomplishments still quote her:

*If you hold your hand closed, nothing good
can come in. The open hand is blessed, for
it gives in abundance, even as it receives.*

These words sum up the way Biddy Mason lived and the principles that guided her. They also explain why she is recalled so fondly many years after her death.

She is remembered best in Los Angeles, where a life that had begun in the misery of the Old South finally ended in the freedom, opportunity, and prosperity of the West. But no matter where Americans live, they can find hope in Biddy Mason's life, her accomplishments, and her rise out of slavery. &

Life and Times

MASON'S LIFE

1818

Born into slavery on
August 15 in Hancock
County, Georgia, and
named Bridget

1810

1812–1814

The United States and
Britain fight the
War of 1812

1823

Mexico becomes
a republic

1821

Central American
countries gain inde-
pendence from Spain

WORLD EVENTS

C. 1848

Gives birth to daughter Harriet; travels with the Smiths from Mississippi to Iowa, then to Utah

1838

Lives as a slave in Mississippi; daughter Ellen is born

C. 1844

Works as a slave for Robert and Rebecca Smith; daughter Ann is born

1845

1836

Texans defeat Mexican troops at San Jacinto after a deadly battle at the Alamo

1846

Irish potato famine reaches its worst

1848

The Communist Manifesto by German writer Karl Marx is widely distributed

MASON'S LIFE

1851

Moves to Southern California with the Smiths and her children

1855

Rescued from moving to Texas with the Smiths

1856

Declared "free forever" by Judge Benjamin Hayes in Los Angeles; works as a nurse and midwife

1855

1852

Postage stamps are widely used

1856

Nikola Tesla, electrical engineer and inventor, is born

1858

English scientist Charles Darwin presents his theory of evolution

WORLD EVENTS

1866

Buys two pieces of property on Spring Street, the first of many she will buy and sell over the next two decades

1865

1862

Victor Hugo publishes *Les Misérables*

1865

Lewis Carroll writes *Alice's Adventures in Wonderland*

1860

Austrian composer Gustav Mahler is born in Kalischt (now in Austria)

MASON'S LIFE

1872

Helps organize
and fund the First
African Methodist
Episcopal Church
in Los Angeles

1875

1873

Typewriters get
the QWERTY
keyboard

1876

Alexander Graham
Bell uses the first
telephone to speak
to his assistant,
Thomas Watson

1869

The periodic table of
elements is invented by
Dimitri Mendeleyev

WORLD EVENTS

1884

Sold property for $2,800 that had been purchased in 1868 for $375

1885

Helps grand-sons start a livery stable

1891

Dies in Los Angeles in January at age 72

1890

1886

Grover Cleveland dedicates the Statue of Liberty in New York, a gift from the people of France

DATE OF BIRTH: August 15, 1818

BIRTHPLACE: Hancock County, Georgia

EDUCATION: Learned skills such as nursing, midwifery, and livestock care from fellow slaves

CHILDREN: Ellen (1838– ?),
Ann (1844–1857)
Harriet (1847– ?)

DATE OF DEATH: January 15, 1891

PLACE OF BURIAL: Evergreen Cemetery, Los Angeles, California

In the Library

Bolden, Tonya. *Rock of Ages: A Tribute to the Black Church.* New York: Alfred A. Knopf, 2002.

Bowen, Richard A. *The African Americans.* Philadelphia: Mason Crest Publishers, 2003.

Diouf, Sylviane A. *Growing Up In Slavery.* Brookfield, Conn.: Millbrook Press, 2001.

Ferris, Jeri. *With Open Hands: A Story About Biddy Mason.* Minneapolis: Carolrhoda Books, Inc., 1999.

Robinson, Deidre. *Open Hands, Open Heart: The Story of Biddy Mason.* Gardena, Calif.: Sly Fox Publishing Company, 1998.

Look for more Signature Lives books about this era:

James Beckwourth: *Mountaineer, Scout, and Pioneer*

Crazy Horse: *Sioux Warrior*

Geronimo: *Apache Warrior*

Sam Houston: *Texas Hero*

Zebulon Pike: *Explorer and Soldier*

Sarah Winnemucca: *Scout, Activist, and Teacher*

On the Web

For more information on this topic,
use FactHound.

1. Go to *www.facthound.com*
2. Type in this book ID: 0756510015
3. Click on the *Fetch It* button.

FactHound will find the best
Web sites for you.

Historic Sites

The First A.M.E. Church
2270 S. Harvard Blvd.
Los Angeles, CA 90018
323/730-7750
To see the home of the oldest black congregation in Los Angeles, founded in the
home of Biddy Mason

Broadway Spring Center
333 S. Spring St.
Los Angeles, CA 90013
213/626-2099
To see the site of Biddy Mason's first home
on Spring Street, a mural of her home and
some of its contents, and a sculpture illus-
trating events of her life

chambers
a judge's private office

congregation
members of a church or religious group

epidemic
widespread outbreak of a disease

expedition
a long journey over land or sea

humanitarian
a person committed to improving the lives
of others

indentured servant
a person bound by contract to work for another
person in return for travel and living expenses

industry
a person's hard work, as well as a type of business, such as the music industry

philanthropist
a person who shows great compassion and love
for humankind

segregation
intentional separation or keeping apart of people
or things

slums
parts of a city where its poorest residents live

testify
to declare something to be true, or declare
something under oath, as evidence in a trial

Chapter 1

Page 14, line 19: DeEtta Demaratus. *The Force of a Feather: The Search for a Lost Story of Slavery and Freedom.* Salt Lake City: The University of Utah Press, 2002, p. 113.

Chapter 2

Page 21, sidebar: Dolores Hayden. "Biddy Mason's Los Angeles 1856–1891." *California History*, Fall 1989, p. 93.

Chapter 4

Page 38, line 15: Kate Bradley Stovall. "The Negro Women in Los Angeles and Vicinity—Some Notable Characters." *Los Angeles Times*, February 12, 1909.

Page 39, line 4: "Chimney Rock: Life on the Mormon Trail" http://www.lds.org/gospellibrary/pioneer/20_Chimney_Rock.html.

Page 43, line 3: *The Force of a Feather: The Search for a Lost Story of Slavery and Freedom*, p. 39.

Chapter 6

Page 60, sidebar: Biddy Mason Collection. University of California, Los Angeles, Research Library, Special Collections.

Page 61, line 3: *The Force of a Feather: The Search for a Lost Story of Slavery and Freedom*, p. 83.

Chapter 7

Page 67, line 13: *The Force of a Feather: The Search for a Lost Story of Slavery and Freedom*, p. 187.

Page 69, line 3: "Biddy Mason's Los Angeles 1856–1891," p. 91.

Page 70, line 2: Ibid., p. 91.

Page 70, line 25: *The Force of a Feather: The Search for a Lost Story of Slavery and Freedom*, p. 111.

Page 72, line 6: Ibid., p. 86.

Page 72, line 17: Ibid., p. 113.

Page 73, line 2: Ibid., p. 113.

Page 73, line 8: Ibid., p. 113.

Chapter 8

Page 77, line 4: "Biddy Mason's Los Angeles 1856–1891," p. 91.

Page 81, line 4: "The Negro Women in Los Angeles and Vicinity—Some Notable Characters."

Chapter 9

Page 85, line 7: *The Force of a Feather: The Search for a Lost Story of Slavery and Freedom*, p. 170.

Page 90, line 9: "Biddy Mason's Los Angeles 1856–1891," p. 97.

Page 91, line 13: *The Force of a Feather: The Search for a Lost Story of Slavery and Freedom*, p. 209.

Page 93, line 9: "Biddy Mason's Los Angeles 1856–1891," p. 99.

Page 95, line 1: Ibid., p. 99.

Biddy Mason Collection. University of California, Los Angeles, Research Library, Special Collections.

Demaratus, DeEtta. *The Force of a Feather: The Search for a Lost Story of Slavery and Freedom.* Salt Lake City: The University of Utah Press, 2002.

Freeman, Judith. "Commemorating an L.A. Pioneer." *Angeles Magazine*, April 1990.

Hayden, Dolores. "Biddy Mason's Los Angeles 1856–1891." *California History*, Fall 1989.

Morison, Samuel Eliot. *The Oxford History of the American People.* New York: Oxford University Press, 1965.

Sigerman, Harriet. *Land of Many Hands: Women in the American West.* New York: Oxford University Press, 1997.

Slaughter, William W., and Michael Landon. *Trail of Hope: The Story of the Mormon Trail.* Salt Lake City: Deseret Book Co., 1997.

Stovall, Kate Bradley. "The Negro Women in Los Angeles and Vicinity—Some Notable Characters." *Los Angeles Times*, February 12, 1909.

Jean Kinney Williams lives in southwest Ohio and has written many books for young readers. She studied journalism in college and has four children. She loves learning about the fascinating people who helped make our country what it is today.

Image Credits